EVERY DAY
with
FOR GROWING

GUIDANCE

BY SELWYN HUGHES

QUIET TIME

When I come to God
with all my questions,
requests, and yes,
sometimes suggestions,
I forget with all these
needs so pressing
just WHO IT IS
I am addressing.
If God is GOD
He can act in love
with just my praise
and not my shove.
At last I see,
my heart understands,
why we're taught to pray
with folded hands!

From *When the Handwriting on the Wall is in Brown Crayon*
by Susan L. Lenzkes.
Copyright © 1981 by The Zondervan Corporation.
Used by permission.

DOES GOD GUIDE?
For Reading and Meditation: Psalm 32:1–11

*"I will instruct you and teach you the way
you should go; I will counsel you with my eye
upon you." (v. 8, RSV)*

Does God really guide and direct the lives of His children? Is it possible to believe that the great Creator and Sustainer of the universe takes a personal interest in the affairs of each one of His people on this microscopic earth? And if so, how does He go about the task of showing us His plans and purposes for our lives? These are the questions with which we shall come to grips in this series of meditations.

A SENSE OF MISSION
Many Christians know little or nothing about personal guidance from God. They go from event to event and live a kind of hand-to-mouth spiritual existence – a spiritual and moral opportunism. They have little or no sense of destiny, or mission. Hence their impact upon life is feeble. Only people who have a sense of mission and who know what it means to be guided by God accomplish things. Without that, life lacks a goal and the dynamic to move towards that goal. If we do not have a sense of being led, we become victims of our circumstances; we are circumstance-directed instead of Christ-directed.

Guidance, as one preacher put it, "is not a spiritual luxury for rare souls but the minimum necessity for every Christian." "Those who are led by the Spirit of God are sons of God" (Rom. 8:14). No leadership – no sonship. Dare to believe it – the Almighty God, at whose word the great planets spin and whirl, condescends to say to you: "I will counsel you with my eye upon you."

*Guidance
is not a
spiritual
luxury.*

O God, forgive me if I have allowed my faith to become second-hand and vague, instead of firsthand and vital. I want so much to know the sense of being led. Impel me from within so that I shall not be compelled from without. Amen.

LIFE IS DULL – WITHOUT GUIDANCE

For Reading and Meditation: Isaiah 58:5–14

"The Lord will guide you always ... You will be like a well-watered garden, like a spring whose waters never fail." (v. 11)

We saw yesterday that if we are not God-led, we shall probably be mob-led. We will react, rather than act. If we are not led by God, then we become led by circumstances, things or people. It is imperative that we Christians regain the sense of being led, for without it life turns dull and insipid.

Recently there came into my hands the report of a conference in the United States where the leading members of a certain denomination were gathered together and asked to share openly and honestly their views on the subject of divine guidance. The conference began with the expected defensiveness, but after a few days the Holy Spirit broke through into the midst of that group with the result that many of them stood up and confessed that they lacked the sense of being led.

WANTING OUR OWN WAY

A minister who was there wrote: "Some of us were well known for our executive ability and efficiency, we were people who were admired by our congregations, but under the scrutiny of the Holy Spirit we were shown to be agitated, half-committed, wistful, self-placating seekers who were more taken up with having our own way than finding God's way. Indeed, many of us came to see that our religion was a second-hand affair, and that our Christian lives were *dull and insipid* (italics mine). We were being guided more by our inner needs than by the constraints of God." Before we become too judgmental, let's pause for a moment and ask ourselves the question: Is my life dull and insipid? Do I lack a sense of being led? I say again, if you are not guided by God you will be guided by something else – by others or perhaps yourself.

If we are not God-led we shall probably be mob-led.

O Father, I see so clearly that to be self-managed is to be self-damaged. Life does indeed become dull and insipid when it lacks Your direction and control. Help me regain the sense of being led. For Your own dear Name's sake. Amen.

STARGAZING IS A SIN

For Reading and Meditation: Isaiah 44:6–22

"... I am the first and I am the last;
apart from me there is no God." (v. 6)

We are seeing, during this first week of our meditations on the theme of guidance, that to be guided by God is imperative, for if we are not led by God we will be led by something else. Of all the things men and women turn to for guidance, astrology is one of the most devastating, for it means that moral considerations have been abandoned and one's destiny is decided by the position of the stars.

Turning to the stars for guidance is always a sign of decay, mentally and spiritually. We are told that several million people in Britain daily consult a horoscope. The newspapers that publish these daily charts are contributing to this moral and intellectual decay.

THE SIN OF IDOLATRY

There is little difference between an ancient pagan bowing before a stone idol, asking for its blessing, and a modern pagan studying charts that depict the movements of lumps of matter in the sky which he thinks guide his life.

My concern here, however, is not so much with secular society, but with those Christians who may be tempted to turn to horoscopes for their daily guidance. Some regard it as an innocent and harmless pastime. This is untrue. The stars which God has made can separate us from Him if we make the stars our guide rather than letting God reveal Himself to us through Christ and His Word. Gazing at the stars in order to find guidance constitutes the sin of idolatry, and must be repented of now – without further delay. Astrology will drain and damage your spiritual life and lead you not toward God, but away from Him.

The stars can separate us from God.

O God, I see how easy it is, when I have lost sight of You, to turn to other things for guidance and direction. I renounce right now every other form of guidance in my life, and put my trust directly in You. Its done, Father. I am Yours to guide. Amen.

"THE CANAAN OF HIS PERFECT LOVE"
For Reading and Meditation: Isaiah 49:1–13

"… He who has compassion on them will guide them and lead them beside springs of water." (v. 10)

I am often asked in letters and in interviews: what is the secret of emancipation from worry? How may one shed a fretful and fearful attitude to life? The answer I usually give is this – *live the guided life*. As soon as one understands the importance of allowing one's life to be guided by God and seeks His direction and control, it is not long before one experiences a deep inner peace.

As Dr. W. E. Sangster put it: "Not to feel the whole burden of responsible decision; not to find one's mind a constant battleground of contending forces; not to be haunted by the fear of the consequences as one anticipates a grave mistake – that is half the journey to the land of inner peace."

PEOPLE OF PEACE

When we are sensitive to the commands and counsel of God, and feel our own powers of reason and insight clarified by the light of His presence, we arrive at what one writer describes as "the Canaan of His perfect love." Here there is still need for toil, but it is toil amid tranquillity; it is the "rest that remains for the people of God" (Heb. 4:9).

Contrast this with the stress and strain of those who feel no co-operative help from above; tossing on seas of uncertainty, and coming to their decisions with frantic and unquiet minds. Indecision then becomes decision. They drift on with a spurious sense of relief, and try to convince themselves that this is the way life should be lived. How different for those who say, "We are not our own; we were bought at a price" (see 1 Cor. 6:19–20). They are the people of peace.

Live the guided life.

O God, quietly I am coming to see that if I live, I must live in You or not at all. You are my Life and my Way of life. When I find Your plan, I find myself, for Your will is my peace. Help me to grasp this even more. Amen.

ANYBODY GOING ANYWHERE?

For Reading and Meditation: Luke 1:67–80

"To shine on those living in darkness ... to guide our feet into the way of peace." (v. 79)

The message I have been trying to get across, in one way and another, during this first week of our meditations, is this – *we Christians must regain the sense of being led*. And why? Because without that sense of being led, life is aimless.

A man stood up at the end of a small Christian conference and said, "Anybody got a car going anywhere?" Everyone laughed, for they knew that a car doesn't just go anywhere – it must go somewhere. Many Christians are just concerned with going anywhere, rather than going somewhere. As long as they are moving, they are not particularly concerned about the direction or the goal. To be successful in our Christian lives, we must not only move, but move in the right direction and in accordance with divine guidance.

GOD GUIDES HIS SERVANTS

I have just been rereading *The Jade Gate*, the story of Mildred Cable and Evangeline and Francesca French who, early this century, travelled to China bearing the good news of the Gospel. It is a wonderful story of hardship and fortitude. Strong men wept when, in 1926, these three women returned home and told their story to the Christians in Britain. Why did they go? Because of guidance: "a secret consciousness of being in receipt of Sealed Orders – to proceed to the great North West to a place at present unknown." Let no one feel, however, that only the great are guided. Our habit of reaching for a classic illustration may sometimes give that impression. God guides more of His servants in the paths of obscurity than He guides in the floodlit way.

Without that sense of being led, life is aimless.

O Father, if my life lacks direction and purpose, then help me to find Your plan for my life, to pay the price of working out that plan, and to make it the adventure of my life. I don't just want to be going anywhere: I want to be going somewhere – with You. Amen.

GUIDANCE WITHOUT GIMMICKS

For Reading and Meditation: Proverbs 4:10–27

"I guide you in the way of wisdom and lead you along straight paths." (v. 11)

We have seen that guidance is the very essence of Christianity – it is not a spiritual luxury for rare souls, but a minimum necessity for every Christian. Now we turn to face an extremely interesting and vital question: if divine guidance is so important and so necessary to effective Christian living, why is it so difficult to obtain?

NO MAGIC FORMULAS

One reason why some Christians find it difficult is because they mistakenly view it as something that can only be obtained by the use of formulas and techniques. Some of the ways Christians adopt to discover God's guidance for their lives are so ridiculous that if they were not employed with such sincerity and devotion, they would be downright hilarious. I heard about a lady, seeking guidance as to whether or not she should go on a Holy Land tour, read in the travel brochure that the flight from London to Tel Aviv would be on a Boeing 747. The next morning she awoke and looked at her clock. It was 7:47 a.m. precisely. This she took as her "sign" from God that He wanted her to go. You may smile at this, but I wonder what methods you adopt in your attempt to discover God's will? God guides – but never by gimmicks. Lest I over-simplify the problem, let me make it clear that there are many areas of legitimate concern that are not specifically addressed in the Bible, and deeply committed Christians are often at a loss to know what to do. However, just as there are no "short cuts" on a straight road, so there are no magic formulas for knowing the will of God.

God guides – but never by gimmicks.

O Father, help me to build clear guidelines for arriving at Your will for my life. Protect me, I pray, from the pitfalls that are ahead, and teach me how to walk in Your paths. For Jesus' sake. Amen.

GOD'S STAMP OF APPROVAL

For Reading and Meditation: John 6:25–40

"For I have come down from heaven not to do my will but to do the will of him who sent me." (v. 38)

We continue examining some of the reasons why Christians find it difficult to get guidance from God. Another reason why guidance fails to come is because, although we may ask God to guide us, what we really want deep down in our hearts is God's stamp of approval on our own selfish desires. I once heard of a man, who prayed this prayer: "Lord, choose me a wife, but let it be Mary." I am not saying, of course, that every decision we make in life has to be submitted to God for His approval, for if that were the case, we probably would never get dressed in the mornings.

HIS WILL NOT MINE

Many of the desires that spring into our minds are tainted with self-centredness and self-interest, and it is perilously easy to bring them to God, not for His examination, but for His unqualified approval. We are like the little boy who prayed that God would make Birmingham the capital of England. When asked why, he replied that he had put it as the capital on his examination paper!

We must fix it in our minds that if we are wanting God's guidance for our lives, then we must be willing to be guided, not to our ends, but to God's ends. A woman was told by her pastor during a counselling session, "Now say to God: 'Let anything happen to me that You want to happen to me.'" She looked at the counsellor aghast: "Oh no," she said, "I don't want that." She thought, as indeed do many Christians, that God's will for her would lie along the line of the disagreeable. The fact is that God couldn't will anything for us except our highest good – and still be God. God's will is in our highest interest at all times, in all places and under all circumstances.

God's will is in our highest interest at all times.

O Father, help me to hold on to this fact – and hold on to it tightly – that Your will is my will at best. So help me seek Your way with my whole being and without reservations. For Jesus' sake. Amen.

GUIDANCE DEMANDS A RELATIONSHIP
For Reading and Meditation: Job 13:1–19

"But I desire to speak to the Almighty and to argue my case with God." (v. 3)

We look at yet another reason why some Christians find it difficult to receive divine guidance – they fail to see that it is difficult to get light in a crisis if you are not willing to get light in the continuous. We must be willing to be guided by God, not merely now and then, but as a life proposition. Perhaps this is why the Bible contains very little specific advice about guidance, but a great deal on the proper way to maintain a loving relationship with our Creator.

Some Christians view God as someone upon whom they call when in a crisis – to get them out of scrapes in which they have become entangled by their own self-will. In the intimacy of marriage, we catch a glimpse of the intimacy longed for by God. God is the Lover, we are the Beloved – therefore the way we communicate is as important as the content of it.

A LAMP TO MY FEET

The plan of your life might be unfolded in a moment of sudden insight, or it might be a gradual unfolding. Yet the gradual unfolding may be the highest form of guidance. Someone said that the text, "The steps of a good man are ordered by the Lord" (Psa. 37:23, AV) means "every two and a half feet". The psalmist said, "Your word is a lamp to my feet" (Psa. 119:105). Note – "a lamp to my feet" – not a spotlight but just enough light by which to see the next step. The advice given to me by one of my tutors in college has never left me: in order to get guidance in a crisis, remain in the will of God in the continuous: "I being in the way, the Lord led me" (Gen. 24:27, AV).

God is the Lover, we are the Beloved.

O Father, save me from being so concerned about hearing Your words of guidance that I overlook the importance of a relationship with You. You are not just my Guide – You are my Father, my Redeemer, my Lover. Help me to remember this – not just some days, but every day. Amen.

PERSONAL DECISION-MAKING

For Reading and Meditation: 1 Thessalonians 3:1–13

"So when we could stand it no longer, we thought it best to be left by ourselves ..." (v. 1)

A further reason why Christians struggle over the question of divine guidance is because they fail to see that, on occasions, God wants us to develop our own decision-making processes.

I speak now of the ordinary perplexities of life when, with a little thought and contemplation, we could think matters through without the active help of God.

DIVINE ABDICATION

C. S. Lewis hinted at God's hesitance to intervene in some situations when he said: "Perhaps we do not fully realise the problem, so to call it, of enabling finite free wills to coexist with Omnipotence. It seems to involve at every moment a sort of 'divine abdication'."

Is it not a secret desire of us all, when faced with some issues that are not covered by the directions of Scripture, to be told in our prayer time exactly what we should do? There are, of course, those blessed occasions when God quite clearly speaks to us and makes known His guidance, but we have to admit that there are other times when He does not. Can it be that on those occasions when no clear direction comes, it is because at that particular moment, in those particular circumstances, our heavenly Father is saying to us: "In the interests of your own personal development, this is something I want you to think through yourself"? (I am speaking here of morally neutral issues, of course. Anything revealed in Scripture needs no further guidance.) Be assured of this, if God hesitates to intervene in your life, it is only because He sees that our ability to make decisions is being impaired by His guidance.

Anything revealed in Scripture needs no further guidance.

Gracious Father, I am so grateful that You have made me a free personality – someone who can make sound moral judgments. Help me to be a responsible and wise decision-maker. For Your own Name's sake. Amen.

THE WILL OF GOD
For Reading and Meditation: Acts 22:1–16

"…'The God of our fathers has chosen you
to know his will.'" (v. 14)

This week we come to grips with the question: does God have an "individual" will for each of our lives? Garry Friesen, the author of the book entitled *Decision Making and the Will of God* (Multnomah Press: USA), claims that the traditional view that God has an "individual" will for our lives is biblically untenable.

Garry Friesen is a committed evangelical who believes wholeheartedly in the authority of Scripture, but by making this statement he stirred up a storm in the Christian community. He describes his book as a "biblical alternative to the traditional view". This raises the question: what exactly is the traditional view of divine guidance?

DIVINE GUIDANCE
Briefly, it runs like this. God's will can be divided into three categories: (1) His sovereign will, (2) His moral will, and (3) His individual will. God's sovereign will is the predetermined plan which He has for the ages, and is always fulfilled. It will not be frustrated by men, angels, or anything else (Dan. 4:35). God's moral will is the plan revealed in the Scriptures, the moral commands which teach us how we ought to live and what we ought to believe. God's individual will is the ideal, detailed life-plan which God has uniquely designed for every believer. This plan encompasses the decisions we make and is the basis of God's daily guidance. These, then, are the three aspects of God's will as accepted by the majority of evangelical Christians, and the view which has been held by most believers throughout the centuries.

A detailed life-plan for every believer.

Father, open my eyes this week to the various aspects of Your will, and guide me by Your Holy Spirit toward the conclusions You would have me draw. I don't just want to know about Your will: I want to know Your will for my life. Amen.

MORE ON THE THREE CATEGORIES

For Reading and Meditation: Daniel 4:34–37, I Thessalonians 4:1–8, Hebrews 13:20–21

"For this is the will of God, your sanctification ..." (1 Thess. 4:3, RSV)

We continue examining the traditional Christian view of divine guidance. God's will, as we saw, can be divided into three categories: His *sovereign* will, His *moral* will and His *individual* will. We can only know as much of God's sovereign will as He permits us to see – as, for example, in biblical prophecy – and usually we recognise it only after it has happened. If something happened in history, it was part of His plan. Many of the older theologians referred to God's sovereign will as His "secret will", contrasting it with His revealed will which we find in the Bible.

KNOWING GOD'S WILL

With regard to the moral will of God, however, it is possible to know not just a part of it, but the whole. The Bible reveals one hundred per cent of God's moral will. You don't need to ask for guidance on the moral will of God, because God has given it in Scripture. If you are thinking about cheating on your income tax so that you can give more money to the work of God, you don't need to ask the Lord's direction – He has already given it. God will never lead you to do something that is against His moral will as revealed in the Bible.

Although the Bible gives general instructions which affect all of life, there is need for guidance in personal matters. For instance, the Bible forbids a Christian to marry a non-Christian, but it should not indicate which particular person one should marry, or for that matter, whether a specific believer ought to marry at all. These personal decisions are influenced by God's moral will, but have to be determined by finding God's individual will.

God will never lead you to do something that is against His moral will.

O God, whose will is inflexibly wrought in history and in the Scriptures, help me to know that same will in every part of my life and being. For Your own dear Name's sake. Amen.

AN ALTERNATIVE VIEW

For Reading and Meditation: I Thessalonians 5:12–28

"... test everything; hold fast
what is good" (v. 21, RSV)

Over the past two days we have examined the traditional view of divine guidance – the view which splits up the will of God into three distinct categories.

We shall now examine the view outlined by Garry Friesen in his book. He argues that the will of God must be seen, not in three perspectives, but two – His sovereign will and His moral will.

PERSONAL PLAN?

There is no biblical support, he says, for the idea of God's "individual" will, and the concept of a personal plan for every Christian's life is not to be found in Scripture. He goes further and says that if he is right, then many believers are investing a great deal of time and energy searching for something that is non-existent. "It simply will not do," he claims, "to assume that God has a unique plan for each life that must be discovered as the basis for decision making."

He concludes that God's moral will, as fully revealed in the Bible, is all that is necessary for a Christian to do the will of God on this earth, and where no specific command or principle is given, the believer is free and responsible to choose his or her own course of action. Whenever the Bible encourages Christians to know the will of God, says Friesen, it is referring to His moral will as already revealed in the Scriptures. Garry Friesen certainly shook up the thinking in evangelical circles on the subject of decision-making (not a bad thing, you might say!) and it will do us no harm to reconsider our position in relation to this compelling thought.

Open my
mind to
truth.

Father, I see that I am going to have to think through this issue very carefully. Open my mind to truth and hold me fast so that I do not get drawn into currents that are contrary to Your Word. In Jesus' Name I ask it. Amen.

FOUR PROPOSITIONS

For Reading and Meditation: I Corinthians 2:6–16

"The spiritual man judges all things, but is himself to be judged by no one." (v. 15, RSV)

W e spend another day familiarising ourselves with the alternative view of divine guidance – the view that states God does not have an "individual" will for our lives, and in searching for it we are looking for something that doesn't exist. In order that you might comprehend this – for, believe me, you are going to come across it sooner   or later – let me state it in the way it is set out in Garry Friesen's book.

PRINCIPLES OF GOD'S WORD

He claims the teaching of Scripture as relating to guidance can be summed up in these four propositions. (1) In those areas specifically addressed by the Bible, the revealed commands of God – His moral will – are to be obeyed. (2) In those areas where the Bible gives no command or principle – morally neutral decisions – the believer is free to choose his own course of action. Any decision made within the moral will of God is acceptable to God. (3) In non-moral decisions, the objective of the Christian is to make wise decisions on the basis of spiritual expediency. (4) In all decisions the believer should humbly submit, in advance, to the outworkings of God's sovereign will as it touches each decision.

The reason why so many Christians are confused when it comes to personal decisions, says Garry Friesen, is not because they are unable to find the "individual" will of God, but because they fail to gain a good understanding of the principles of God's Word. Knowing those principles, he claims, allows God to work within a believer, enabling him to make good and wise decisions.

Humbly submit to the out-workings of God's sovereign will.

Father, help me to be open in my mind, to listen, consider, and even to change my ideas when the change is in harmony with Your Word. This way I grow – the other way I remain stunted. Amen.

DRAWING TOGETHER
For Reading and Meditation: Ephesians 4:1–16

"So that we may no longer be children, tossed to and fro and carried about with every wind of doctrine ..." (v. 14, RSV)

Now that we have pulled the two main views concerning divine guidance into focus, it is time to ask ourselves: which is right? The fact is that both of them contain a degree of truth, but the truths need to be drawn together to form a more complete whole. Although I do not agree with some of Garry Friesen's conclusions, I am appreciative of his contribution, because he has made me – and, I know, many others – rethink our position in relation to this important matter.

What, then, is the strength and the weakness of the alternative view? Its strength lies in its emphasis on the need to absorb the principles of Scripture, so that we learn to make wise spiritual decisions in matters that are outside the scope of the Bible. Its weakness is its failure to recognise that God directs His children, not only through the Bible, but also through the witness of His Spirit speaking directly to their hearts.

TRADITIONAL VIEW
The strength of the traditional view is its insistence that God does have an "individual will" for each of His children: its weakness, however, is its claim that God wants to be involved in every one of His children's decisions – no matter how trivial or unimportant. God is interested in the tiniest details of our lives, but He does not want us to look to Him for guidance on every decision we are called upon to make. If God's "individual" will covered every single detail of our lives – the shoe we should put on first in the morning – our personalities would soon become stunted and cramped. God wants to guide, but not to override us.

God is interested in the tiniest details of our lives.

Father, give me a wise and understanding mind so that I can see the strengths and weaknesses in the arguments of men. Guide me by Your Holy Spirit so that I might formulate clear convictions and beliefs. In Jesus' Name I ask it. Amen.

For Reading and Meditation: Matthew 6:5–15

"Your kingdom come,
your will be done ..." (v. 10)

We spend one final day answering the question: does God have an individual will for each of His redeemed children? Despite the insistence of the alternative view that God does not have a personal will for His people, it is quite clear – to me at least – that the Bible claims He does. For centuries, men and women have sought the promised guidance and testified that God was as good as His word. The Bible is full of such stories. Look into the Old Testament: think of Abraham's servant finding Rebekah, of the stories of Moses, Samuel and the prophets – all wit-nessing to the fact that God's guidance is particular as well as general.

The same can be seen in the New Testament also. Think of Philip and the Ethiopian eunuch, or of Ananias and Saul, or of Peter and Cornelius. And what of the example of Jesus? He got His guidance, not only from Scripture, but from direct contact with God in prayer. How did He know how to be in the right place at the right time? He was guided. He taught His disciples to pray, "Your will be done" – a prayer which presupposes the possibility of knowing that will; and knowing it, one must assume, not as a mass of vague sentiment, but with some concreteness and precision.

In each generation, godly people have claimed that the disciplines of Bible reading and prayer have led them to know God's guidance in their lives. Augustine and Luther, St. Teresa and Wesley – these and countless others vouch for its truth. Be assured of this – your Father has a unique and personal plan for your life.

Your Father has a unique and personal plan for your life.

Father, I'm convinced – You do have a personal will for my life. If You have any word of guidance to give me this day, help me to heed it. Give me discernment to hear Your Word above all other words. Amen.

GUIDANCE THROUGH THE WORD

For Reading and Meditation: 2 Timothy 3:10–17

"All Scripture is God-breathed and is useful for teaching, rebuking, correcting and training in righteousness." (v. 16)

It is time now to come to grips with the question: how does God guide us? "How – how do I find God's will for my life?" From here on, I will attempt to put the "how" into the subject of guidance.

How, then, does God go about the task of steering us toward His perfect will and purpose for our lives? He does it primarily through His Word, the Bible. *Scripture provides the single most important guide and checkpoint for our lives.* I love the way the Living Bible translates the text at the top of the page: "The whole Bible was given to us by inspiration from God and is useful to teach us what is true and to make us realise what is wrong in our lives; it straightens us out and helps us do what is right."

GOD'S WORD

There are many verses in Scripture which emphasise that God's Word is the major checkpoint for our lives. Paul tells us in Galatians 1:6–9 that even if an angel were to supernaturally appear whose message contradicted the already revealed will of God in the Scriptures, one should hold to the Bible rather than the angel's message. The Jews of Berea were commended in Acts 17:11 for listening to Paul's preaching with open and attentive hearts, and then checking the Scriptures to see if what was spoken was correct. In the Scriptures God has given us 66 books filled with principles and precepts which provide a much more objective set of guidelines than those that come from impulses or feelings. And the better we know His Word, the more clearly we will know His will.

The better we know His Word, the more clearly we will know His will.

O God, I am so grateful that You have not only spoken in the Bible, but that daily You speak through it. Help me to hide Your Word in my heart so that it becomes the mainspring of all my actions, determining my conduct and my character. Amen.

THREE IMPORTANT STEPS

For Reading and Meditation: John 8:21–36

"… 'If you hold to my teaching, you are really my disciples. Then you will know the truth, and the truth will set you free.' " (vv. 31–32)

We said yesterday that the better we know God's Word, the more clearly we shall know His will. Unfortunately, a person may intellectually know what the Bible says, and may even have memorised it from cover to cover – yet still be oblivious to its real meaning. If he has not "made it his own" through obedience to it, he won't even understand what the Bible is all about. I have met men with theological degrees who know all about the history, geography and literary merits of the Bible, but who had no more idea of its inner message than, as we say, "the man in the moon".

UNDERSTAND THE TRUTH

There are three steps we must take to profit from God's Word. Step one is to *hear the truth*. This means that you have to do more than just read these notes – you must read the Bible itself. Step two is to *believe the truth*. This means accepting its message as from God. Step three is to *practise truth*. This means doing whatever God asks you to do, whether you feel like it or not. The Amplified Bible's rendering of verse 31 in the passage above reads: "If you abide in My Word – hold fast to My teachings and live in accordance with them …"

Hear the truth. Believe the truth. Practise the truth.

The result of these three steps is understanding the truth, and when we understand His truth we are better able to understand His will for our lives. Note, however, that full understanding comes only *after* obedience. Our lives must be guided by God's Word, checked at every point by His Word, fed by His Word and characterised by obedience to His Word. Then, and only then, are we in a position to specifically seek God's will and guidance regarding any particular issue.

O Father, help me to catch the wonder of the fact that the more I steep myself in Your thoughts as they are revealed in the Bible, the more I shall be fired by Your passion and imbued with Your decisiveness. Amen.

For Reading and Meditation: 2 Corinthians 1:12–22

"I planned to visit you on my way to Macedonia and to come back to you from Macedonia ..." (v. 16)

Today, before going on to consider how to use God's Word correctly in guidance, we pause to consider how it is often incorrectly used. Many Christians use their Bible like a lucky dip. This is often referred to as the "finger-pointing method".

This practice of opening the Bible at random and receiving the first word one reads as a personal divine message has brought about much harm. Although God sometimes uses random opening of the Bible to speak to His children, it must never become a substitute for close study and perusal of the Scriptures.

SELF-WILL TO GOD'S WILL

Another caution to bear in mind is the tendency some Christians have to make the Bible mean what they want it to mean. This is why we can never understand the Bible correctly until we are willing to submit our own will and desires to the will of God. If we don't, then we can very easily see in a text only that which supports our self-centred ends. The cults do this all the time. Guidance cannot come until the self is surrendered, and the life is shifted from self-will to God's will. Don't be tempted to think the end justifies the means, and misuse passages to gain your own ends, rather than God's ends.

Be careful, too, of the danger of always wanting a Bible text to support every decision you make. Some Christians say: "Search the Bible for a word which exactly fits your situation, and never do anything until you have one." It is good to have a firm Scriptural basis, but the idea of always being able to find a specific verse which is exactly applicable to any given situation leads to a distortion of Scripture.

Guidance cannot come until the self is surrendered.

O Father, help me to curb any tendency to try to make the Bible mean what I want it to mean. I see that guidance cannot come until I turn from wanting my own will to wanting Your will. My will shall be Your will. I surrender – now. Amen.

DAILY DISCOVERIES IN THE WORD
For Reading and Meditation: Psalm 119:129–144

"The entrance of your words gives light;
It gives understanding to the simple." (v. 130, NKJV)

We are seeing that the Bible is God's chief way of guiding and directing His people toward His will for their lives. How, then, shall we read the Bible to get the maximum guidance from its pages?

First, we must study it with *prayer*. As we take it in hand, let us remember that this Book was written by men who were specially guided by the Holy Spirit, and it will only be understood, in all its richness, by those who have the same divine help.

DAILY READING OF THE SCRIPTURES

Second, we must read it every day – *unhurriedly*. Of course, as I have said so many times before, we must not get into bondage about this and think that if we miss one day's Bible reading because of some emergency, God is going to withdraw His presence from us. Remember God is your Father – would any human father act like that? But do make it a goal to read it every day in a relaxed and unhurried way. You are most receptive when you are relaxed. Nothing can be inscribed on a tense and anxious mind. Little value can be derived from a chapter hurriedly scanned, and the mind diverted at once to something else.

Third, ask yourself two vital questions in relation to every verse or passage you read: what did it mean when it was first written? What does it mean for me now? Sometimes the two answers will coincide. Sometimes the answer to the first question will elude you, and yet the passage can still have personal worth. Nobody who seeks divine guidance can neglect the richest and surest way to it – the daily reading of the Scriptures.

You are most receptive when you are relaxed.

O God, You have breathed into the words of Scripture and they have become the Word. Help me to saturate my thinking and my inner motives with Your mind, until I cannot tell where my mind ends and Your mind begins. Amen.

SWEETER THAN HONEY!

For Reading and Meditation: Psalm 119:97–112

"How sweet are your words to my taste,
sweeter than honey to my mouth!" (v. 103)

We continue looking at how to study the Bible for pleasure and profit.

Fourth, learn how to retain key passages of Scripture by committing them to memory. I was in a church some time ago when a young man reading the lesson spoke these words: "You shall hate all men for my name's sake." One or two lifted their eyebrows, but most of the congregation showed no surprise. Most of them, I concluded, didn't know the correct reading, which is "You shall be hated of all men for my name's sake." I am more and more concerned that the generation in which we are now living seems not to be trained in memorising Scripture – and it is mentally and morally the poorer as a result. May I make a suggestion? Over the next seven days, commit a verse to memory each day, and see if your spiritual life is not the richer. Don't just take any text of the Bible, but select one that has a special and personal meaning for you.

MEDITATION

Fifth, if some verse or passage speaks to your condition, then roll it round and round in your mind – this is called "meditation". Turning Scripture over and over in your mind enables the Word of God to produce an atmosphere within your soul. The atmosphere becomes an attitude, and the attitude soon becomes an act. When Jesus was hard-pressed by the temptations in the wilderness, He answered in the words of Scripture. The words He used had become part of Him, and in the crisis they naturally passed from the stage of assimilation and atmosphere to that of attitude and act.

Commit a verse to memory each day.

O Father, how I long to be able to think as You think, feel as You feel and love as You love. Yet the answer is before me: I must meditate in Your Word. I shall begin today. Help me to continue. Amen.

For Reading and Meditation: I Peter 1:10–24

"… they spoke of the things that have now been told you by those who have preached the gospel to you…" (v. 12)

We spend one more day looking at how to read the Bible. Sixth, let the Bible lead you to Christ's feet. Reading the Bible is not merely an intellectual exercise – it is a tryst with the Trinity. I heard a minister tell how he was sitting in a train one day reading the Bible, when a bright-faced oldish lady opposite him blurted out, "Oh, you must love the Author, for you are reading His Word. I, too, love the Author." "At once," he said, "we were friends around *the* Friend. In reading the Word, remember that what you have read is leading you to His feet. Upon Him all the Old Testament truths converge: from Him all the New Testament truths emerge. He is the centre of gravity of the Bible; look for Him when you are reading its pages."

PUT INTO PRACTICE

Seventh, as you read the Word, keep re-aligning your life with Christ's life. In Korea, a girl did not come back for more instruction in Scripture and when asked why, she replied, "I haven't learned to practise fully what I have been taught." She felt she had to keep abreast of the teaching – and she was right.

Eighth, if something gets hold of you when you are reading Scripture, pass it on to someone else – the same day. I stressed this point several years ago in my writings, and a woman wrote to me and said: "That was the best piece of advice I have ever received in my whole life. I learned that I never fully understood a truth until I shared it. In the sharing the meaning and impact become more real." Repetition helps retention, and what is more – it helps brighten the path of another.

Pass it on to some-one else.

O Eternal Word, may my words this day be but echoes of You. My words are dead unless there is spirit in them – and You are that Spirit. Speak to me that I may speak to others. For Your Name's sake. Amen.

MADE IN HIS IMAGE

For Reading and Meditation: Genesis 1:20–31

"So God created man in his own image, in the image of God he created him ..." (v. 27)

ast week we said that the Scriptures provide the single most important checkpoint in our lives. The Bible is the cornerstone of guidance, and the more we know and understand God's Word, the more effectively we can be guided.

Before we go on to see how biblical principles can operate in our lives to help us correctly decide things that are not covered by Scripture, we pause to consider the issue of individual freedom. How much freedom does God give us in making decisions over things that are outside the scope of Scripture? The way we perceive our individual freedom has a direct bearing on our views concerning guidance.

NOT ROBOTS

When God created man He made him in His own image. That image accounts for man's great value to God and distinguishes him from all other creatures. Man alone was invested with the determinative features of personality – intellect, emotion and will. And only man was given a position of responsibility requiring the exercise of those attributes. If we were to make our decisions based on instinct – as do the animals – we would be no different from them. Or if we required direct input from our Creator for every decision we are called upon to make, then we would be no more than manipulated robots. One writer puts it like this: "By God's design, only the image-bearer (man) approaches decisions in the same manner as the Creator." What a risk God took in making us like Himself. Inevitably. But He took it. God, being the loving Being He is, could not do otherwise.

Man's great value to God.

Father, I stand astounded at Your courage. You could have made me in such a way that I would have had to obey Your will – yet You made me a free and independent being. Voluntarily I lay my will at Your feet and confess my greatest freedom is in being bound to You. Thank You, Father. Amen.

FREEDOM – NOT UNLIMITED

For Reading and Meditation: Romans 2:1–13

"All who sin apart from the law will also perish apart from the law, and all who sin under the law will be judged by the law." (v. 12)

We saw yesterday that man, made "in the image of God", makes decisions, not as a function of instinct, as do the animals, but in the same manner as the Creator Himself – by conscious choice. Dr. John White, in his book *The Cost of Commitment*, puts it most effectively when he says: "Within boundaries prescribed by God's own character, man analyses, evaluates, judges and freely *determines* (italics mine) his choices."

The principle of freedom of choice was clearly part of the Creator's design from the very beginning. Adam and Eve were free to partake of any of the fruit that grew in the Garden of Eden, with only one restriction: "But from the tree of the knowledge of good and evil you shall not eat" (Gen. 2:17, NKJV). In this very first commandment man's freedom to choose was categorically asserted, and provided in advance a rebuttal of Satan's allegation that God is a tyrant (Gen. 3:1–5).

PRESCRIBED BOUNDARIES

The freedom that man has, however, is not an unlimited freedom. People are free, of course, to go beyond the limits set by rules or law, but they are not free to choose the consequences of their actions. Once they have misused their freedom in transgressing the prescribed boundaries, then they have to face the consequences of their actions. We are free only within certain limits. You are perfectly free, for example, to jump off the roof of a ten-storey building, but after you have jumped you are no longer free – you will be caught in the grip of gravity and brought swiftly to the ground. So mark this and mark it well: you are free – but free only within limits.

You are free only within limits.

O Father, how can I thank You enough that in Your wisdom, You have put limits on my freedom. Help me to understand this and work within the boundaries You have set, and not try to operate outside them. Amen.

FREEWILL OFFERINGS

For Reading and Meditation: Leviticus 22:17–33

"… If any of you … presents a gift for a burnt offering to the Lord, either to fulfil a vow or as a freewill offering" (v. 18)

We are meditating upon a matter which to some might seem academic and irrelevant, but take my word for it – you will never be able to understand divine guidance until you understand the issue of individual freedom. Man was given the freedom to make free judgements, but he was also given the dignity of bearing full responsibility for the consequences of his choices. God said to Adam "in the day that you eat of it you shall die", and precisely as God said, Adam died spiritually the moment he sinned, and he began also to die physically.

PRINCIPLE OF FREEDOM

Does that mean that after Adam sinned, the principle of freedom was revoked? No. It did require, however, a more extensive revelation of God's moral will and character. The human heart is now tainted with sin, and has a bias that moves it away from God – so the area of freedom becomes more restricted as the limits of God's moral will are set out.

The principle of freedom, although more constricted and narrowed down as a result of Adam's sin, remained in force even under the Law. Take the example of the freewill offering which is before us today. A man could ask: "Is it God's will for me to give a freewill offering today?" If God answered, then the offering would no longer be one of freewill. God wanted to give His people some way in which they could express their voluntary devotion to Him. So He provided the option of the freewill offering and explained which sacrifices would be acceptable for this purpose.

The human heart has a bias that moves it away from God.

O Father, forgive me that so often I wait until You have done something for me before I bring you my offering of thanks and praise. Help me to give you more freewill offerings – praise that is not squeezed out of me, but rises freely because it must. Amen.

COME TO DINNER!
For Reading and Meditation: I Corinthians 10:23–33

*"So whether you eat or drink or whatever you do,
do it all for the glory of God." (v. 31)*

Quietly we are coming to the conclusion that the principle of freedom was not only established in the Garden of Eden, but continued – with greater restrictions because of sin – after the Fall. Examples are abundant. Perhaps the clearest evidence of this can be seen in relation to food.

The subject of food – a matter of importance in the Garden of Eden, as well as in ancient Israel – reappears as a topic for discussion in the early Church. A question had arisen in the Corinthian church in relation to eating meat that was sold in the market place after it had been offered to idols. Was this an issue about which there was a definite divine command? No. Then how was a believer to act if he accepted an invitation to a meal from an unbeliever, and then suspected that he was being offered idol meat?

EAT ANYTHING
Notice Paul does not say, "If an unbeliever asks you to come to dinner, pray about it and determine whether it is God's will for you to go", but rather, "If one of the unbelievers invites you, and you wish to go, eat anything that is set before you, without asking questions for conscience' sake" (v. 27, NASB). A believer is free to accept or decline an invitation but once he makes the decision to go, he is then under a Scriptural obligation not to probe the meal's pedigree or recent history for the sake of his conscience. Since there is no moral issue involved with the eating of the meat itself, the Christian is free to make up his mind whether or not to accept an invitation, but not free to refuse the meat on the grounds that it offends him (v. 25).

Is this an issue about which there is a definite divine command?

Father, the more I study this question of individual freedom, the more I see that You are not abandoning me to my own devices, but reaching out after me and awakening me to new levels of maturity. Help me to be a wise decision-maker – one whose decisions always glorify You. Amen.

LIKE A FATHER
For Reading and Meditation: Psalm 103:1–22

"As a father has compassion on his children, so the
Lord has compassion on those who fear him" (v. 13)

W e have been seeing that although God surrounds us with clear guidelines and prescribed limits, within those limits we are accorded a good deal of personal freedom.

In the days when horses were taken down into the coal mines, usually the driver, or leader, would walk the horse and lead it wherever he wanted it to go. This close leading of the horse, however, took away its initiative and the horses tended to lose their spirit; they became helpless and over-dependent. To correct this, every now and again they had to bring the horses up to the surface and allow them to run free. In this way they regained their spirit and recovered some of their initiative.

INDEPENDENTLY DEPENDENT

God won't weaken us by imposing Himself upon every decision we have to make. He guides – but not in a way that cripples our initiative. Take another illustration – the father who takes his child's development seriously seeks to give him or her as wide a scope as possible for the exercise of judgment and decision-making. He is quick with words of counsel, which his love and experience qualify him to give, but as the child grows and develops, they come to a time when they need less and less of their father's active counsel and support. The father who does everything for his child, dictating every least thing they should do throughout the day, weakens, not strengthens, that child. We, of course, as God's children, can never grow beyond His help, but He does want to develop us so that we learn to be independently dependent.

He guides – but not in a way that cripples our initiative.

Father, drive this truth deeply into my spirit before I move on – that I am created to be independently dependent. Like an earthly parent, You are teaching me how to make wise decisions, but unlike an earthly parent, there will never be a time when I can do without You. Thank You, Father. Amen.

AN IMPORTANT GUIDING PRINCIPLE
For Reading and Meditation: Colossians 3:12–25

"Let the word of Christ dwell in you richly as you teach and admonish one another with all wisdom."
(v. 16)

N ow that we have firmly established the fact that there is a good deal of freedom in life, we move on to consider the question: how can we make sure that our free decisions are the right ones? There are some who say that in an area which has no clear Scriptural principle governing it, you should go ahead, make the best decision you can, and whatever you decide will be acceptable to God. It is part of your freedom, they say, to make some choices on your own, and at such times you must not wallow in indecisiveness, but make up your own mind based on the options before you.

SPIRITUAL PRINCIPLES
That seems like good advice as far as it goes, but it leaves out an important factor. While it is true that God allows us a good deal of freedom in life, we must seek to exercise this freedom with a sense of responsibility. No Christian should adopt the attitude, when he faces a situation which is not covered by a verse or passage in the Word of God – such as: Whom shall I marry? What vocation should I choose? etc. – that he can make his decision without recourse to any spiritual principle.

There is one principle which takes precedence over all others when it comes to decision-making in areas that are not directly covered by Scripture, and that principle is contained in a word which appears in the Bible, in various forms, over five hundred times. I'll identify it for you tomorrow, but in the meantime, try to refrain from turning to the next page and see if you can spot it in today's Scripture passage.

Exercise this freedom with a sense of responsibility.

Gracious Father, help me to know and discover this seemingly important principle that has been hinted at today – not only in the passage, but in myself. Whet my appetite to know more and more of the Bible's truths. For Your own Name's sake. Amen.

"LIFE: GOD'S VIEWPOINT"

For Reading and Meditation: Colossians 1:1–14

"… we have not ceased to pray for you and to ask that you may be filled with the knowledge of His will in all spiritual wisdom …" (v. 9, NASB)

Did you spot the word that defines the guiding principle which undergirds our decision-making processes in areas not covered by the Word of God? Then here it is – *wisdom*. God wants us to develop spiritual wisdom so that when we are faced with decisions in the non-moral areas of our lives, we are able to make wise and prudent choices.

WISDOM

What is wisdom? J. B. Phillips gives an excellent perspective on it when he translates Colossians 1:9 in this way: "We are asking God that you may see things, as it were, from His point of view by being given spiritual insight and understanding." Wisdom can be defined quite accurately as "seeing things from God's point of view". Dr. J. I. Packer gives the following definition: "Wisdom is the power to see, and the inclination to choose, the best and highest goal, together with the surest means of attaining it." Wisdom, quite simply, is the ability to figure out what is the best thing to do in any given situation.

So how do we go about acquiring wisdom? I should point out at this stage that the Scripture identifies two types of wisdom that we need to cultivate – *spiritual* wisdom and *supernatural* wisdom. Spiritual wisdom comes from assimilating the truths and principles of Scripture; supernatural wisdom comes through the miraculous intervention of the Spirit in our lives. We shall look a little later at the subject of supernatural wisdom – but right now, let's begin our quest for spiritual wisdom by opening our hearts to God in this special prayer:

Wisdom is the ability to figure out what is the best thing to do.

Gracious Father, I come to You with the utmost humility and ask You to make me a wise person. I need so desperately to be able to see life from Your point of view. Show me the steps that are necessary to attain spiritual wisdom, and help me to take each one – with no drawing back. Amen.

STEPS IN GAINING WISDOM
For Reading and Meditation: Proverbs 8:1–21

"I love those who love me, and those who seek me find me." (v. 17)

We continue focusing on the question: how do we go about the task of acquiring spiritual wisdom? Our text for today tells us that those who seek it shall find.

Firstly, where do we find it? The major source of spiritual wisdom lies in soaking oneself in the Scriptures. Let there be no mistake about this. Spiritual wisdom is not the result of good training or the learning of techniques; it comes from exposing oneself to the wisdom that flows through every page of the Scriptures. I have known believers, highly trained in the skills of decision-making, who made huge blunders in their Christian lives. They had plenty of knowledge, but lacked wisdom. One definition of wisdom says that it is "the ability to put knowledge to its best effect".

STUDY REQUIRES EFFORT

The process of gaining wisdom, as we shall see, contains a number of elements, the first of which is exposing our minds to God's eternal Word. We talked earlier about the importance of reading God's Word – and reading daily – but now we must go one stage further and emphasise the importance of *studying* the Word of God. Study requires effort, but the effort in turn produces spiritual wisdom. Few Christians, it seems, are willing to put an effort into serious study of the Bible. They make do with devotional aids such as this, but have no form of systematic study by which they "search the Scriptures". I sincerely hope this study will help you in your devotional life, but quite honestly, I feel it fails if it does not prod you toward a more diligent study of the Word of God.

Soaking oneself in the Scriptures.

O Father, help me to organise my life so that I can give more time to diligent study of Your Word. Sometimes my life gets cluttered with the extraneous and the non-essential. Show me how to rearrange my priorities. Amen.

WISE UP!

For Reading and Meditation: Proverbs 9:1–18

"The fear of the Lord is the beginning of wisdom, and the knowledge of the Holy One is understanding." (v. 10)

We continue looking at the Scriptures as the fount of spiritual wisdom. It is every Christian's responsibility to get to know as much about the Bible as they can. This includes reading (1 Tim. 4:13), careful consideration (2 Tim. 2:7), searching and enquiry (1 Pet. 1:10–11), diligence in study (2 Tim. 2:15), meditation (Psa. 1:2), memorisation (Psa. 119:11) and learning from gifted Bible teachers in both oral and written form (Phil. 4:9; 1 Cor. 12:28–29; Gal. 6:6). The more we do this the more the wisdom of this wonderful Book will be absorbed into our spiritual bloodstream.

THE VALUE OF WISDOM

Spiritual wisdom does not flow from a mere study of the Scriptures – it comes only as we *obey* it. "Do not let this Book of the Law depart from your mouth; meditate on it day and night, so that you may be careful to do everything written in it." (Josh. 1:8). The second step in obtaining wisdom is to develop the attitude that wisdom is so valuable you will do everything humanly possible to obtain it. Reflect on the fact that as far as spiritual things are concerned, no man is wise in himself (Prov. 3:7). Our attitude must mirror the conviction that the source of wisdom is God alone. If we do not admit this, then we are self-deceived fools (Rom. 1:21–22). Wherever you look in Scripture, you will find that the attitude of the one who receives wisdom is that of reverence, humility, diligence, uprightness and faith. The man or woman in whom wisdom is found is a person who bows humbly at the feet of the Creator.

No man is wise in himself.

O Father, I frankly confess that You are the source and fount of wisdom. I bow before You again this day and ask that You will make me a walking expression of Your eternal wisdom. This I ask in Jesus' Name. Amen.

MORE STEPS TO WISDOM

For Reading and Meditation: James 1:1–12

"If any of you lacks wisdom, he should ask God, who gives generously to all without finding fault ..." (v. 5)

Did you get the first two steps in obtaining wisdom, which I have been sharing with you, firmly in your mind? Briefly, here they are again. (1) Read, study and meditate in the Word of God; and (2) develop a proper attitude toward the importance of wisdom.

PRAY

Today we come to the next two steps for getting wisdom. (3) Pray for it. It is true that God's major way of imparting wisdom is through His Word, the Bible, but it is not His only way. He gives it also through the avenue of believing prayer. (4) The fourth step in obtaining wisdom is to look out at life. The author of Proverbs – the textbook on obtaining wisdom – makes the point that God has built wisdom into nature, and that people would do well to reflect on the things which animals do by instinct (see Prov. 30:24–28 and Job 12:7–8).

The importance of obtaining wisdom by observing the habits of certain animals has been greatly overlooked by the Christian Church. The wisdom that God gave to Solomon included a thorough understanding of the world of nature (see 1 Kings 4:33–34). Adam's first task in the Garden of Eden was to name each animal as God brought them to him. He would never have been able to give them precise names if he had not thoroughly understood their ways. In Scripture God assumes that we know the ways of animals. If we do not know something of the behaviour of bears, we will never appreciate nor understand the warning, "Better to meet a bear robbed of her cubs than a fool in his folly" (Prov 17:12).

God has built wisdom into nature.

O Father, what a thrilling thought! – Your wisdom shines, not only in Your Word, but in the world that is around me. Help me to be a good observer of the lessons You have hidden in Your creation. For Jesus' sake. Amen.

GET HELP WHEN YOU NEED IT

For Reading and Meditation: Proverbs 15:1–23

"Plans fail for lack of counsel,
but with many advisers they succeed." (v. 22)

We come now to our fifth and final step in obtaining wisdom – *discuss important issues with a wise spiritual counsellor.* The book of Proverbs stresses the importance and value of wise counsellors to the decision-maker. In seeking to add to your wisdom – and especially before making an important decision – talk the situation over with a wise and caring Christian friend.

The kind of person you should look for is one who has the reputation of possessing deep spiritual insight, and who has gone through a good many relevant experiences. Incidentally, if you want to be a counsellor, then be prepared to face all kinds of problems, because it is in the "University of Adversity" that God trains His counsellors (see 2 Cor. 1:4).

RIGHT DECISIONS

Let's now try to sum up what we have been saying over this past week before we move on to consider other aspects of our theme. We began by asking: how can we be sure that our free decisions are the right ones? The key, we discovered, lies in obtaining spiritual wisdom. God's chief way of imparting His wisdom to our minds is through His Word, the Bible. The more we study it – and obey it – the more the wisdom from this wonderful Book flows into our spiritual bloodstream.

God mediates His wisdom to us in other ways as well – through the development of right attitudes, through prayer, through nature, and through the counsel of wise and mature Christians.

Talk the situation over with a wise and caring Christian.

O God, my Father, from the depths of my heart I ask again that You will teach me how to be a wise decision-maker. As I follow the steps You have shown me this week, develop in me true spiritual wisdom. For Your own dear Name's sake. Amen.

DO CIRCUMSTANCES GUIDE?

For Reading and Meditation: Jonah 1:1–17

"But Jonah ran away from the Lord and headed for Tarshish ..." (v. 3)

Over the past few weeks we have been stressing the fact that the Bible is God's chief method for guiding and directing our lives, and when called upon to make decisions that are not covered by a biblical statement or passage, we apply to such decisions the wisdom we have derived from our exposure to God and His Word.

The question we now ask ourselves is this: what other forms of guidance does God use to help us when we come to a crossroads and don't know which way to go? One way is through *circumstances*. A Christian knows that God is sovereign over all things, and that He can work in and through circumstances to bring about His will. At times, therefore, God will bring about unexpected, unlikely circumstances together with precise timing to reveal His will.

CIRCUMSTANCES CAN MISLEAD

Circumstances by themselves, however, should not be accepted as clear indications of God's will, for some circumstances can mislead us, rather than lead us. When God spoke to Jonah to go to Nineveh and tell the people to repent, the prophet took a route that led in the opposite direction. Circumstances seemed right for his escape – he found a ship going to Tarshish and discovered he had just the right fare. Some believers I know, whose lives are guided only by circumstances, would have said: "God must have changed His mind. He doesn't want me to go after all. Look, things are coming together perfectly." Circumstances should be looked at carefully, subjected to much prayer and discussed, if possible, with a wise and experienced fellow believer.

God is sovereign over all things.

Father, it is so easy to believe what I want to believe. Teach me not to fall for anything that happens, hook, line and sinker – but to weigh everything carefully and prayerfully. Give me the wisdom to discern between circumstances that lead and those that mislead. Amen.

THE INNER VOICE

For Reading and Meditation: John 10:1–20

"My sheep listen to my voice; I know them, and they follow me." (v. 27)

Today we consider the guidance that comes through the witness of the Holy Spirit speaking directly to our hearts. In the first scene of Bernard Shaw's *Saint Joan*, Captain Robert de Baudricourt pours scorn on Joan's belief that she has heard a heavenly voice by saying, "Such voices come from you imagination." Joan's reply was this: "Of course; that is how the messages of God come to us."

Is that how God speaks to us? Through the imagination? I think not. Thousands of believers who have made a practice of listening to God claim they can distinguish between their own imagination and the impress of God's will. This comes, they say, as the result of long practice. The more we develop the "listening" side of prayer, the more our spirits are sensitised to hearing God's voice.

A WORD OF CAUTION

Here, again, I must add a word of caution. Many years ago I thought God had spoken to me about a certain issue, and I rested my whole weight on it – and it let me down. My faith was shaken, but not shattered. I recognised that the voice I had heard was the one I *wanted* to hear; it was my own subconscious giving me what it knew I deeply desired. An exception like this does not discredit the principle, however. Nowadays I am more careful and because of that, more accurate in recognising God's voice. God does guide through an inner voice, but such guidance is given only to those who have practised quiet and patient waiting on Him, and know how to disentangle the voices of the subconscious from the voice of God.

Develop the listening side of prayer.

Lord Jesus, You who lived in such a close relationship with Your Father that His gentlest whisper was like thunder in Your ears, help me to have that same consciousness – that same responsiveness. For Your own dear Name's sake. Amen.

GOD GUIDES THROUGH REASON

For Reading and Meditation: Ephesians 4:17–32

"... be constantly renewed in the spirit of your mind – having a fresh mental and spiritual attitude" (v. 23, Amplified Bible)

Wouldn't it be wonderful if all we had to do to be guided was simply to sit down quietly in God's presence and listen for His voice? It sometimes happens that way, but experience shows that it is not a fixed pattern. Sometimes God guides us through our mental processes, through hard thinking and reasoning.

I heard of a minister who received a "call" to another church, and took the matter to the Lord in prayer. The impression he got was that he must think it through, issue by issue and point by point. Speaking of the experience afterwards he said, "The more I reasoned, the clearer the issues became." And when a Christian is called upon to find God's guidance through reason, how much easier this is if our mind-set has been developed through consistent exposure to the principles of God's Word by daily reading, study and prayer.

Sometimes guidance comes through a small fellowship group whose members are committed to each others' spiritual growth. I am thankful that increasingly, in churches of all denominations, believers are coming to see the importance of functioning together in small groups. It is not uncommon for our spiritual eyes to have "blind spots", and one of the gains of functioning in a committed group is that the things we cannot see ourselves can be pointed out and put right.

If God cannot guide us when we are alone – perhaps because of our insensitivity or defensiveness – then He sometimes resorts to guiding us through a group. One way or another, He will get His message across to us.

One way or another He will get His message across.

O Father, I see again the advantage of developing a spiritual mind-set. Then, if guidance has to come through the way of reasoning, it will come with greater ease and understanding. Thank You for the brothers and sisters You have given me to support and strengthen me in Your cause. Amen.

GUIDANCE THROUGH DESIRES

For Reading and Meditation: Philippians 2:1–13

"For it is God who works in you to will and to act according to his good purpose." (v. 13)

A nother way in which God sometimes guides is along the line of our personal desires. The thing we long to do is often the thing God wants us to do. Many Bible teachers avoid even mentioning this form of guidance because it is so obviously fraught with problems. However, let's think our way through them together.

COMPLEX PROBLEM

One problem we can fall into is what is known as the "filthy rags" complex. The Bible says that our righteousness is like "filthy rags", and some people assume from this that every single desire we have is a selfish one. If such a person really wants to do something, he is checked by the thought that because he wants to do it, it is a selfish desire and cannot be God's will. It doesn't always follow, however, that a desire springing up in our heart is a selfish one – it *could* be a definite prompting of the Spirit.

Another problem in relation to our desires is what is often called the "identical twins" theory – which is the exact opposite of the "filthy rags" complex. This is based on Psalm 37:4, which says: "Delight yourself in the Lord and he will give you the desires of your heart". Some Christians take this verse to mean that if they are really dedicated to the Lord, then their desires will always be identical with His desires. This view is inviting because it is always easier to determine our desires than to discover the Lord's will. The proper approach is a balance between the two. You should not think of your desires as being "filthy rags" or "identical twins", but as something in between – they need to be looked at, carefully considered, and prayed over.

The thing we long to do is often what God wants us to do.

O Father, help me to know the difference, I pray, between the selfish desires that rise up in my heart and those that come from You. Prune my heart until Your will and my will coincide. For Your own dear Name's sake. Amen.

THE OPENING OF OPPORTUNITIES

For Reading and Meditation: Deuteronomy 29:29

"The secret things belong to the Lord our God,
but the things revealed belong to us ..."

God guides also through bringing us up against some opportunity or need. Many years ago on the streets of London, a little waif sidled up to a man and said: "Do you want to see where we live?" The man assented, and went with the little waif into some alleyways where some boys were sleeping in boxes – huddled together to keep one another warm. The man sat there most of the night, and before morning came, he knew he belonged to those boys. His name was Barnardo, and he went on to set up the internationally famous Dr. Barnardo's Homes. God's guidance was the opening of the doctor's eyes to see an urgent need.

TO REALLY SEE

It's amazing how all around us there are needs which we look at with our eyes, yet do not see – that is, really see. There comes a moment, however, when it seems as if the scales fall away, and the need takes on a perspective of which you were previously unaware. I do not believe, as do some, that the need is the call. I have looked upon many areas of need in my time, and wished that I had the ability and the capacity to meet them all, yet as I have prayed I have been led to focus on those areas of need to which I am best able to contribute.

In bringing you face to face with a need or an opportunity, the Spirit will quicken your imagination, and create a concern in your heart from which you cannot escape. When that happens, it is almost certain you are being guided.

All around us there are needs.

O God, open my eyes to see all needs, but particularly the ones You want me to see. I want to be guided into something that takes up all my energy, my faith and my love. Lead me on – I will follow. In Jesus' Name. Amen.

WHEN AN ANGEL GUIDES

For Reading and Meditation: Acts 12:1–17

"Suddenly an angel of the Lord appeared ... He struck Peter on the side and woke him up ..." (v. 7)

We consider one more avenue through which God gives guidance – the supernatural – such things as supernatural dreams and visions, the appearance of angels, miraculous interventions or manifestations of the gifts of the Spirit such as the word of wisdom, prophecy and so on.

Some Christians believe, of course, that supernatural guidance was given only to the early Church, and that after the initiation period described in the book of Acts, supernatural events and happenings were no longer needed. The view I have always taken on this matter is as follows: although God's usual way of guiding His people is through His Word, and in many areas not covered by Scripture, by the impartation of spiritual wisdom, He does, at times, use supernatural means of guidance.

THE SUPERNATURAL

I have witnessed in my own life occasions when God has guided me through such supernatural things as prophecy, dreams and the word of wisdom. However, honesty compels me to admit that it has not been a normal, everyday occurrence. The same cautions must be applied to supernatural happenings that we applied to other means of guidance – namely, that if a supernatural event does not line up with the revealed will of God in Scripture, then it must be ignored. That means if an angel taps you on the shoulder and commands you to do something which is contrary to the Word of God – forget it. God uses many forms of guidance, but the one authority by which all guidance is to be evaluated is, as we have been at pains to point out – God's eternal and infallible Word.

God does, at times, use supernatural means of guidance.

O Father, the more I study this subject of guidance, the more I realise the value of Your Word, as contained in the Bible. May all my decisions fit into its perfect pattern. For Jesus' sake I ask it. Amen.

SOME PREPARATORY QUESTIONS
For Reading and Meditation: Romans 12:1–21

"Therefore, I urge you, brothers, in view of God's mercy, to offer your bodies as living sacrifices ..." (v. 1)

We come now to the final stage of our journey in seeking to discover the biblical principles that underlie the subject of Guidance. Our task from here on is to pull together the principles we have been examining in order to develop a strategy for discovering God's guidance in those areas of our lives which are not directly covered by a clear statement of Scripture. Keep in mind, however, that step-by-step answers and checklists will never eliminate our need to walk by faith, keeping our eyes on Christ.

OUR LORD AND SAVIOUR
The steps I am about to give you are ones that I use in my own life to determine divine guidance, but before I do so there are several preparatory questions I must ask you. Firstly, are you a Christian – one who knows God personally through faith in Christ? The steps I am going to give are "family" principles that can only be applied by members of God's family. If you are not a Christian, then surrender your life to Christ right now. Bow your head, ask God to forgive your sin and invite Christ into your life to be your Lord and Saviour.

Secondly, are you in good health – physically and emotionally? If not, then you may have difficulty applying these guidelines with the level of sensitivity that is needed. You may need the help of your minister or a Christian friend in determining divine guidance. Thirdly, are you willing to do God's will when once it is clear to you? Settle this issue right now, for only those who are willing to do His will can fully know it.

Walk by faith, keeping our eyes on Christ.

O God, forgive me for any hesitancy I may feel in relation to Your perfect will. Why should my eye be afraid of light, my stomach pinched with hunger, afraid of food? No more should I be afraid of Your will. I will not be. Amen.

LISTEN, LEARN, OBEY ...

For Reading and Meditation: Ephesians 6:10–18

"Pray at all times in the Spirit, with all prayer and supplication ..." (v. 18, RSV)

W e have one more issue to face before we begin laying down some guidelines for determining divine guidance. Do you regularly spend time with God in prayer and in the reading of the Scriptures? If you don't, then you will lack one of the most essential elements for understanding divine guidance – *spiritual sensitivity and wisdom.*

Assuming that you are a Christian with fairly good health, that you are willing to do God's will once it is shown you and you regularly spend time with God in prayer and reading His Word, we are now ready to focus on the steps we need to take when seeking to know God's will in matters that are not clearly covered in Scripture.

FULL ALERTNESS

First, begin by praying that God will help you discern and discover His will. Since God has an individual purpose for each life, we must become skilled in the art of finding out what that purpose is. When you pray for guidance, therefore, cultivate these three attitudes – listen, learn, obey. Some of us listen but won't learn, and some of us learn but won't obey. A dedicated Christian is one who listens, learns and obeys. If he does not, there will soon be nothing to listen to, or to learn, or to obey. "Prayer", said someone, "is an imperative part of seeking God's will. It does for you what a garage mechanic does when he cleans the windscreen of your car. It allows you to see the road and the signs without distortion or distraction." Prayer, also, is like a rush of cool air from a rolled-down window. It brings the drowsy driver back to full alertness.

Pray that God will help you discern and discover His will.

O God, unconnected to You I am like a dead wire; but attached to You I throb with energy and glow with light. Make my connection with You so sure that I shall always stay plugged in to Your endless supply. In Jesus' Name. Amen.

THE SPIRIT AS OUR GUIDE

For Reading and Meditation: John 16:1–15

"... when he, the Spirit of truth, comes,
he will guide you into all truth ..." (v. 13)

We are examining the steps we need to take when attempting to discover God's guidance in matters where there is no clear scriptural command. Step number two is this: open your heart in willing submission to the Holy Spirit and invite Him to be your Counsellor and Guide.

THE SPIRIT AND THE WORD

The two greatest means of guidance God has given us are the Bible and the Holy Spirit. We have already emphasised the relevance of Scripture in the matter of guidance, so today we focus on the person of the Holy Spirit. The Bible is our objective authority – the Holy Spirit our subjective authority. Throughout the centuries, the Church has always endeavoured to keep these complementary authorities in balance – the Spirit and the Word.

Some Christians place all their emphasis upon the Word. Thus they fall prey to an arid intellectualism and rationalism; they have little sense of the Spirit's presence in their lives. For others it is the subjective experience alone that counts. They rely so heavily upon the Holy Spirit that the Bible, apart from a few proof texts, becomes a neglected book. These believers have no operative objective authority in their lives. Both positions are wrong. If you tell me the Holy Spirit is leading you in a certain direction or to a certain decision, I have a right to insist that you check this out with the Scriptures. I assume you have absolute confidence in God's Word – that is good. Now open your heart to the Spirit so that He might flow into you and through you to give the help and guidance that you need.

Open your heart to the Spirit.

Gracious God, give me a perfect balance between the Spirit and the Word. With all Word and no Spirit, I dry up. With all Spirit and no Word, I blow up. With both Word and Spirit – I grow up. Father, I want to grow. Help me – for Jesus' sake. Amen.

GENERAL PRINCIPLES
For Reading and Meditation: I Corinthians 6:9–20
"Flee from sexual immorality ..." (v. 18)

We come now to the third step: see if you can find a Biblical principle that clearly relates to the issue which is before you.

The Bible contains both precepts and principles. A precept is a clear and specific statement that takes all guess-work out of the situation – for example, today's text. Sexual immorality is never the will of God – never! But the Bible also contains principles – general guidelines – that assist us through the "grey" areas.

SOME PRINCIPLES
Some principles to employ in decision-making are these: Is my motive to bring glory to God? (1 Cor. 10:31) Will what I am planning to do make me more effective for Christ? (Col. 3:17) Will my decision cause another Christian to stumble? (Rom. 14:21) Will it involve me in any kind of evil? (1 Thess. 5:22) Will it hinder or help my growth toward spiritual maturity? (Heb. 12:1) Will it compromise me and affect my Christian testimony? (Eph. 5:11)

There are scores of such principles in the Bible – so get to know them. From now on, make a list of every biblical principle you come across in your reading. Then, when you are next faced with a difficult decision, the Holy Spirit will use your knowledge of the Scriptures to lead you to an awareness of how His general principles apply to your particular question or difficulty. As a Christian yielded to the Spirit of God, your conscience and spirit will respond, and you will know one thing at least – whether or not the matter is in line with God's Word.

Make a list of every biblical principle you come across.

O God, help me to store up in my spiritual storehouse such a supply of biblical principles that I will be able to draw upon them in those times when I am uncertain of the way ahead. This I ask in Jesus' Name. Amen.

For Reading and Meditation: Psalm 37:1–24

"Delight yourself in the Lord and he will give you the desires of your heart." (v. 4)

The fourth step one can take in relation to the matter of divine guidance is this – ask yourself: is the issue that I am facing in line with my own personal desires? In terms of guidance, this has great implications. It means that I don't have to distrust all my own feelings and inclinations. If you are daily walking with God then, in general, your feelings, inclinations and ideas may well be Spirit-inspired. I say "may well be" because those feelings must be checked alongside the other guidelines I am presenting.

TIME HAS A BEARING

Step number five is this: realise that the more important the decision you have to make, the more time should be given to it. Insignificant and unimportant issues ought to be decided quickly. Big and far-reaching ones should be looked at a little longer, and all the issues carefully weighed up. Give yourself a deadline for the task.

This is what I sometimes do: I take a sheet of paper, and draw a line down the centre of the page. At the top of the left-hand column, I write the word "Pro", and at the top of the right-hand column the word "Con". I then prayerfully consider and write down all the positive aspects, then negative aspects of the issue, listing them in the appropriate columns. I might even consider a 24-hour fast, with prayer and meditation in the Scriptures, which greatly increases the sensitivity of the human spirit. When the decision has to be made, I go ahead and make it on the basis of what I have considered is best.

I don't have to distrust all my own feelings.

Father, I am so grateful that when I am living close to You, Your will and my will coincide. Deliver me from all emotional blockages that would unbalance me, and deepen my relationship with You. Teach me how to be a decisive person. Amen.

LISTEN TO OTHERS

For Reading and Meditation: Proverbs 20:1–15

"The purposes of a man's heart are deep waters,
but a man of understanding draws them out." (v. 5)

Today we come to step number six: if God's guidance is not becoming clear to you, then consider talking the matter over with a wise and experienced fellow-Christian.

The wise king Solomon wrote: "As iron sharpens iron, so one man sharpens another. As water reflects a face, so a man's heart reflects the man" (Prov. 27:17 and 19). When Moses was in difficulty because he couldn't cope with his increasing responsibilities in governing the Israelites, he received some wise advice from Jethro, his father-in-law. Jethro said: "You and these people who come to you will only wear yourselves out. The work is too heavy for you; you cannot handle it alone" (Ex. 18:18).

NEGLECTED MINISTRY

Almost everywhere we look in Scripture, we find passages that highlight the fact that believers ought to help and admonish one another. Listen to this: "Let the word of Christ dwell in you richly as you teach and admonish one another with all wisdom ..." (Col. 3:16). Young Christians ought almost always to check their guidance with an older and more experienced believer. Older women in the Church are told to instruct and encourage the younger women (Tit. 2:3–5). I know the references above relate to teaching and sharing the principles of God's Word, but I think they could also mean the talking over of personal problems and issues such as decision-making and guidance. But how often is this done? Sadly, it is a greatly neglected ministry in the Church. Make no mistake about it – God uses others to help us know His desires.

Help and admonish one another.

Gracious Father, I am so grateful for all those who have come into my life with a kindly word and deep insight. Perhaps today it might be my turn to be the agent of Your mind to someone. If so, then I shall be deeply grateful. Amen.

For Reading and Meditation: I Corinthians 16:1–14

"But I will stay on at Ephesus until Pentecost, because a great door for effective work has opened to me ..." (vv. 8–9)

We look now at step number seven: look to see if God is saying anything in and through your circumstances. Since circumstances provide the context in which many decisions have to be made, they are a key source of information to the Christian who is seeking guidance.

COINCIDENCES

They must be evaluated, however, not on their own, but in line with other aspects of God's leading. Christians who depend on circumstances alone to guide them can fall into difficulties. Amazing coincidences happen every day – to Christians and non-Christians alike – and we must learn to "read" our circumstances aright, for, as we saw with Jonah, they do not always convey God's direction for our lives. This is why I say again, circumstances should be laid along-side other aspects of guidance – the inner witness, the principles of Scripture, the guidance of others and so on.

Be careful about attempting to set up situations in order to find guidance. One woman I know who wanted guidance on a certain matter said to herself: "If tomorrow morning the milkman leaves two bottles of milk instead of the usual one, then I will take it as God's will that I should become a missionary." This is taking guidance through circumstances too far! It is legitimate, I believe, *along with other guidelines* to look for God's direction through circumstances – but circumstances, because they can so easily be misread, must be only a part of guidance and not the whole.

Be careful about attempting to "set up" situations.

Gracious heavenly Father, give me the spiritual insight and sensitivity I need to be able to "read" my circumstances aright, and use them, along with other guidelines, to arrive at the right conclusions. For Jesus' sake. Amen.

SUPERNATURAL GUIDANCE

For Reading and Meditation: Acts 16:1–15

"During the night Paul had a vision of a man of Macedonia … begging him, 'Come over to Macedonia and help us.'" (v. 9)

We continue meditating on some of the steps we can take when we are unsure about God's guidance. Step number eight is this: keep in mind that when spiritual guidance does not seem to make your pathway clear, God is always able to resort to supernatural guidance.

VISIONS AND DREAMS

I define "spiritual guidance" as the guidance that comes through prayer, meditation in the Scriptures, reasoning, etc., and to "supernatural guidance" as the things God does to guide us which are outside His ordinary and usual methods. I refer to such things as visions, dreams, and so on. I strongly suspect that God works in supernatural ways when He is having trouble getting through to us along the usual channels – although I can't be entirely certain about that.

An interesting example is the vision that Paul received in the passage before us today, which brought about a change of his plans. You would think that if anyone planned his future in a spiritual way, it would be Paul. But here he seems to be moving in a direction other than what God has planned for him, and so the Holy Spirit intervenes supernaturally and spectacularly to direct him into a new sphere of activity. It was exceptional guidance, and obviously not the kind that was an everyday occurrence in the life of the great apostle. I can think of a number of times in my life – and so, I am sure, can you – when in facing a situation that was unclear, God finally revealed His purpose to me in a supernatural way. Let us never forget we are serving a *miraculous* God.

Never forget we are serving a miraculous God.

O Father, forgive me for forgetting that, if need be, Your guidance will get through to me even if You have to use the spectacular means to do it. Yet let me not use that assurance to neglect that ordinary means of guidance which are always at hand. For Jesus' sake. Amen.

THE WAY OF PEACE

For Reading and Meditation: Colossians 3:1–15

"And let the peace (soul harmony which comes) from the Christ rule (act as umpire continually) in your hearts ..." (v. 15, Amplified Bible)

The ninth important step to take when seeking divine guidance is this – learn the secret of a sanctified and properly used imagination. It's interesting, as C. S. Lewis once observed, that in relation to most spiritual issues Christians seem to fall into one of two extremes – either of taking things too far, or not far enough. Some Christians use their imagination too much and magnify their fears and uncertainties out of all proportion. Others fail to use their imagination at all, and thus are bereft of an important aspect of guidance.

IMAGINATION

Whenever you are faced with a situation in which there are several possible options, and after applying the other methods I have suggested you are still not certain which way to go, then try what is often called "the way of peace". Get alone with God, and prayerfully commit your way to Him. Then, in your imagination, go down each of the roads which are open to you. Visualise yourself in each of the various situations and see if you can determine in which one you experience the most peace.

Learn the secret of a sanctified and properly used imagination.

When we prayerfully apply our imagination to several options that are open to us, providing we are living in accordance with God's revealed will in the Bible, we can fully expect Him to flood our hearts with peace when we travel along the right option in our imagination. This method, when used alongside the other methods I have suggested, is a valid means of supplementary guidance.

O Father, I see again how important it is to maintain a daily devotional contact with You. It sensitises the compass of my life so that the needle will point in the right direction – the direction of peace. I am so thankful. Amen.

For Reading and Meditation: Hebrews 11:1–16

"... without faith it is impossible to please God ..." (v. 6)

A final step we should take in determining guidance is to remind ourselves of the fact that God never makes the path ahead absolutely clear because He wants us to exercise faith. This applies not only to the unrevealed will of God, but also to His revealed will as laid out in the Bible.

Many of the challenges God gives us in His Word require an act of faith and obedience before we can actually experience them in our lives. When I first read Romans chapters 6 and 7, and came across the principle of "reckoning myself dead to sin", I thought it was the most ridiculous thing I had ever heard. I remember saying to myself: how can the benefits of Christ's death on Calvary come to me simply by "reckoning" on it? Yet as I took that principle by faith and acted on it, in an amazing way the light came on in my heart.

ACT OF FAITH

Sometimes the same thing happens in relation to guidance in the unrevealed areas of my life. I come to a point where I believe all the road signs are pointing in a certain direction, but then a doubt or an uncertainty creeps in and I am afraid to move. At such times I remind myself of this last principle, and providing I have checked out the other means of guidance, I take a step of faith into the unknown and trust God. The knowledge of God's will – both His revealed and unrevealed will – always calls for an act of faith, as in obedience we move out into what, in some measure, is uncharted territory. How gratifying it becomes, however, when we look back in retrospect and say: "Yes, truly, God led me. That decision was most definitely His will."

God wants us to exercise faith.

O Christ of the undaunted faith, give me, I pray, Your quiet confidence and courage. May I not hold this faith: may it hold me – hold me when everything else fails. For the glory of Your peerless Name I ask it. Amen.

A WORD OF ENCOURAGEMENT

For Reading and Meditation: Psalm 73:17–28

"You will keep on guiding me all my life with your wisdom and counsel; and afterwards receive me into the glories of heaven!" (v. 24, TLB)

On this last day of our meditations on the subject of Guidance I feel God wants me to make the final word a word of encouragement – perplexing as many of the problems are, and partial though our explanations may have been. In all great effort there comes a testing time, and in living the guided life, it comes again and again.

The discipline of daily prayer times may chafe you – especially during those "dry" periods which come to everyone – but the discipline must be endured in the sure knowledge that guidance, in its highest form, comes most clearly to those who soak their thoughts in God's Word and enjoy constant communion with Him.

LED BY GOD

But do not just think of the discipline – think of the rewards. Is it not wonderful to walk through life feeling the certain pressure of His guiding hand? Is it not wonderful to be assured of the fact that, whether in sunshine or shade – He leads me? Is it not wonderful also to experience the security of knowing that, even when we might have made a wrong decision because of our human frailty, God is able, given our consent and co-operation, to bring our lives back on to the right course?

Walk through life feeling the certain pressure of His hand.

Amazing Love! How can it be? Take heart, my friend – the future need not frighten you. As you give your whole attention to the things that make you most responsive to His guidance, striving above all else for a greater sensitivity to His will, seeking you will find, and finding you will follow Him to the end – and beyond the end, where

*The invisible appears in sight
And God is seen by mortal eye.*

Father, You have shown me the way – now help me to walk in it. Teach me to live in harmony with the central purpose of my existence, so that I can say, as did Your Son: "I have finished the work that You gave me to do." Amen.